FRANK Sinatra

AMERICAN ✷ ICONS

FRANK Sinatra

CARA STEVENS

An imprint of Globe Pequot

Distributed by NATIONAL BOOK NETWORK

Copyright © 2018 The Rowman & Littlefield Publishing Group, Inc.

British Library Cataloguing in Publication Information available

Library of Congress Cataloging-in-Publication Data available

ISBN 978-1-4930-3300-3 (hardcover)
ISBN 978-1-4930-3301-0 (e-book)

Cover and interior design by Vertigo Design NYC

♾ The paper used in this publication meets the minimum requirements of American National Standard for Information Sciences—Permanence of Paper for Printed Library Materials, ANSI/NISO Z39.48-1992.

Printed in the United States of America

Contents

From the very moment he entered the world, Frank Sinatra was bigger than life.

Early Years

SUNDAY, DECEMBER 12, 1915
415 Monroe Street, Hoboken, New Jersey

Dolly Sinatra, a tiny, feisty, nineteen-year-old mother-to-be, lies in pain on her family's kitchen table in a small tenement flat in Little Italy. She and husband Marty are happy that their first child is almost here, but things aren't going well with the birth, and Dolly is suffering.

When the doctor arrives, it is apparent that the lives of both mother and child are in jeopardy. He employs a pair of obstetrical forceps to help free the child, but in his haste—perhaps in a panic over Dolly's increasingly deteriorating condition—the physician rips the baby out, tearing open the left side of its face, ear to cheek to neck. He places the blue, bloody, lifeless newborn on the counter next to the sink and returns his attention to Dolly. While his efforts do manage to save her life, the trauma renders her infertile.

While the physician attends to Dolly, her quick-thinking mother proves unready to give up on the child. Despite the clear physical damage, and in the absence of any sign of life, she picks up the 13-pound bundle and washes it in cold water directly from the tap in an old-fashioned attempt to startle the infant to life. Then magically, with a soft shake and a pair of smacks on the bottom, little Francis Albert Sinatra breathes and stirs. Then, he wails his first note.

What a beautiful note.

Frank as a Child

A SHARP DRESSER WITH A CLEAN PUNCH

Frank Sinatra's mother had planned for a daughter, so a very young Frank toddled the harsh streets of Hoboken dressed in pink frilly clothing, which helped to toughen him up at an early age. He soon graduated from girly clothes to sharp suits and ties. As a kid who dressed like a businessman, he still stood out, but he owned his look with pride.

His parents were Italian immigrants. They were hard workers, always busy—often too busy to spend time with their son. As a consequence, Frank grew up independent but lonesome. He often regretted the fact that he never had siblings to play with as a child, though he spent time with his cousins, aunts, and grandmother who lived nearby.

His father worked as a dockworker, prizefighter, and fireman. He boxed under the name Marty O'Brien because Italians weren't welcome in the boxing world at the time. He and his wife, Dolly, an amateur singer and also an immigrant from Italy, owned a tavern called Marty O'Brien's.

Frank was supposed to be named Martin, after his father. A confused priest accidentally named him after his godfather, Frank Garrick instead. His mom didn't mind, and stuck with the name.

A SWEET CHILDHOOD MEMORY

Frank's mother had been an amateur opera singer in her youth. When Frank was three, his mother, Dolly, had every kids' dream job: she worked in a chocolate factory.

"I remember my first visit to the candy store. She had a bucket of ice water and a vat of hot, fudgy chocolate. She dunked her hand in the icy water and then the hot chocolate, which stuck to her fingers. From the book *Frank Sinatra: My Father*: She was a chocolate dipper, who decorated the chocolates with identifying letters. She gave me three pieces of chocolate. It was wonderful."

The Teenage Years

SCARFACE

As a teen, his nickname was "Scarface" thanks to a combination of run-ins with local bullies, scars from his traumatic birth, and a bout with cystic acne. As an adult, he wore makeup to hide it, but more often than not, he turned his right side to the camera to hide his scars.

At school, Sinatra was rowdy, unhappy, and often got into trouble. But in the evenings at the tavern, young Frank would climb up on top of the piano and sing to the customers. He was happiest when he was performing, whether he was doing celebrity impressions for his classmates or crooning for the tavern patrons.

"Mom kept physically fit chasing me and whacking me around now and then. But my mother wasn't tough; the neighborhood was tough. She wanted me to be safe, to be a gentleman. She would have had me wear velvet pants, I think, except that, when we lived on Monroe Street, I would have gotten killed. The funny thing about the Park Avenue neighborhood was that the guys there were worse than the guys downtown. They were brighter, more insidious; well mannered, with good clothes—and deadly."

In his early teen years, he and his friends often cut class and never did homework. He actually cut school for an entire year before his mother found out. At the age of fifteen, Frank officially left high school. He attended a semester at business school to satisfy state requirements, then happily closed the door on his formal education and went off into the world to find his place as a performer.

"Guys would throw pennies and try to get them into my mouth. But I used to move a great deal so they couldn't hit it. It was great fun."

Becoming the Hardest-Working Man in Show Business

Frank's father wasn't happy he left school. "He wanted me to go to college in the worst way," Frank recalled. "He was a man who could never read or write his name and his big point was education." The year was 1932. It was the heart of the great depression and times were tough. Jobs were hard to come by and almost all of them involved manual labor. Frank tried a few different jobs down at the shipyard where his father worked, but none of them suited him. He decided he'd try to earn his living doing what he loved best: singing.

Since his father wouldn't allow him to quit his day job, Frank spent days working down at the shipyard and nights singing with combos and getting gigs anywhere he could. Frank brought his own "sound system" with him—a megaphone like Rudy Vallee used. He finally borrowed money from his parents to buy a real sound system with a microphone and sheet music. That added the style and professionalism he needed to get the edge over other amateurs vying for gigs.

SUMMER OF LOVE: On a hot summer night in 1935 down at the Jersey Shore, Frank met his first love, Nancy. Nancy's father was adamant that Frank earn a living. "No job, no Nancy," he would say. So Frank went to work for her father, plastering walls. He worked hard, but didn't take to the work. He was also exhausted from performing nights and working all day, so he occasionally fell asleep on the job! He eventually quit, but continued to sneak Nancy out on the sly for dates.

THE HOBOKEN FOUR
AND MAJOR BOWES

BIGGER THAN BING CROSBY

One night in 1935, on a date with Nancy, Frank saw his idol, Bing Crosby, on stage in New Jersey. He knew at that moment he had to become a singer.

Frank worked harder than ever after that, playing every gig he could land even if he made little or no money. Sometimes he was paid in sandwiches or cigarettes, but Frank played for the love of the music, the adoration of the crowd, and the dream of one day becoming more famous than Bing Crosby.

Frank played for the love of the music, the adoration of the crowd, and the dream of one day becoming more famous than Bing Crosby.

Sinatra's first broadcast appearance was with the band on the popular radio show "Major Bowes Amateur Hour." It was the first ever reality show, where contestants traveled from far and wide hoping to catch their big break, many selling their homes and hopping freight cars across the country for their shot at stardom. Ten thousand people applied each week and only 20 made it on the air. Most were gonged and laughed off the stage before finishing their acts, but Frank and his band, who had been discovered by an agent for the show, took top prize: a six-month contract to perform on stage and on the radio.

The members of The Hoboken Four: James "Skelly" Petrozelli, Fred "Tamby" Tamburro, Patty Prince, and Frank "Slats" Sinatra.

He attracted the notice of a local group named The Three Flashes, who invited him to give up his solo act and join them. The Three Flashes became The Hoboken Four. They landed a gig playing at the Hoboken Union Club in their hometown. It wasn't quite stardom, but Frank knew it was only a matter of time.

Breaking into the Business

FRANK SANG FOR JUST $1 A WEEK

On the road, Frank missed his girl, he missed his family, and he missed performing solo. He left the Hoboken Four and returned home, pounding the pavement across New Jersey and New York City, and taking any gig where he could sing to an audience or on the radio. He eventually worked his way up to eighteen spots a week on WNEW radio, getting paid less than $4 a month.

GOOD AT BUILDING HIS BRAND

Frank hadn't done well at school or at the manual labor jobs he tried, but when it came to building his name and talent as a singer, his business smarts were right on the money. He hired a diction coach for $1 a session to help lose his Jersey accent. The coach recognized his naturally great vocal range, and encouraged him to test the limits of what he could do and expand his range. Frank also had professional photos taken, and went to great lengths to get his pictures out to local bandleaders. Joining a big band was the pinnacle of success in those days, and that was Frank's goal. He

SWINGING WITH THE BIG BANDS

The Legendary Rustic Cabin: In 1939, Frank landed a job singing, waiting tables, and joking with customers at the Rustic Cabin, a local hangout near where he still lived with his parents. The site broadcast nightly performances over local radio station WNEW, where people would tune in from homes across the area. This was no accident. Frank was looking to expand his reach outside of his small world of Hoboken, New Jersey, and he hoped bandleaders, talent scouts, agents, and anyone else with a good ear and ties to the industry would discover his voice on the radio. Local clubs would broadcast the radio station as well, and Frank was amazed to learn that people were listening to his music and dancing the night away all over the New York metropolitan area. Locals weren't the only ones tuning in. Up-and-coming bandleader Harry James had seen Frank's promotional photos come across his desk. When he heard Frank on the radio he was impressed.

"You Want the Singer, You Take the Name": Harry James came down to the club and offered Frank his first big break as a professional singer, with one caveat: he thought "Sinatra" was "too Italian" and wanted to bill his new protégé as "Frankie Satin." According to a witness, Sinatra's famous blue eyes went cold as he refused, telling James "You want the singer, you take the name."

Many recording studios had gone bankrupt in the wake of the 1929 stock market crash and Great Depression, but big band jazz survived and thrived through broadcast radio. Sinatra sang with James's for a couple of years, performing locally and broadcast over radio. He recorded ten songs with James and his orchestra, but money was tight and James' band wasn't taking off as quickly as Sinatra wanted it to.

Career Takes Flight

HOW FRANK GOT DISCOVERED

When Frank heard the famous bandleader Tommy Dorsey was going to be visiting his old haunt the Rustic Cabin in New Jersey, Frank made it a point to show up and take the stage that night. Dorsey didn't know it at the time, but this was Frank Sinatra's big audition. Tommy Dorsey took the bait, and hired him soon afterward. At 24 years old, after nine years of struggling, his dreams were finally starting to come true. Harry James graciously let Frank out of his contract, and Frank went on to pursue his own dream of fortune and fame as a bandleader.

The Tommy Dorsey Years

A relationship built on mutual admiration and jealousy: Sinatra traveled the country, singing and performing with Dorsey and his band for two years. He recorded 40 singles with RCA in 1940 and an additional 29 singles on the same label in 1941. But as Sinatra's popularity soared, Dorsey started to feel upstaged. Frank began to think about heading out on his own and going solo.

SINATRA GOES SOLO

Emmanuel "Manie" Sacks, the head of Columbia Records at the time, caught his act and told Frank how much he liked his music. Frank dared to ask if he liked it enough to record him as a solo artist. Sacks agreed heartily and offered to record him as soon as he was ready. It meant waiting out his contract with Dorsey and RCA, but Frank kept his eyes on his future and bided his time. Unfortunately, he had to wait a long time and put up a big fight to get out of his iron-clad contract. Leaving the band meant the controlling Dorsey would get 48 percent of Frankie's take for life. Depending on whom you ask, it either took three threatening ruffians or a determined lawyer, a talent agency, and $25,000 to extricate Sinatra from his obligations to Dorsey, but eventually, Frank was free to go off on his own.

SINATRAMANIA

Something about Sinatra's voice made young women melt. Hordes of teens in their pencil skirts and ankle socks screamed and tried to touch him at his concerts.

DECEMBER, 1942, PARAMOUNT THEATRE, NEW YORK CITY: Frank's first fans of his solo act were planted in the audience by Sinatra's publicist, George Evans, and were paid $5 each to scream as loudly as they could to drum up fervor in the crowd. The teens swarmed the theater and went absolutely wild when he took the stage. "The sound that greeted me was absolutely deafening," Sinatra recalled years later. "I was scared stiff. I couldn't move a muscle."

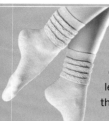

Fans were forced to remove their shoes when they danced so they wouldn't scuff the floors at the clubs. They danced in their ankle-length "Bobby socks," which gave them their name: **BOBBY SOXERS**

With many of the young men off to war, Sinatra's popularity with the ladies soared. His piercing blue eyes, open stance, and earnest way of singing made it seem as if he was singing directly to each member of the audience. Critics and parents weren't so sure about this skinny, big-eared kid, but the girls were completely enchanted.

Dangerous swarms of love-struck teens stalked Sinatra everywhere he went. Frank Sinatra's adoring fans weren't always the harmless teenagers they appeared to be. Frank was forced to hire extra security to sweep his hotel rooms before he entered so he wouldn't be accosted by fans hiding under the beds, behind the drapes, or in the closets. Fans often swarmed the artist as he exited trains, buildings, or cars, often causing damage in the process and scaring the daylights out of Sinatra and his entourage. "It was exciting, but it scares the wits out of you, too," Sinatra recalled.

Frank was born just across the river in Hoboken, but his love for NYC was deep and mutual.

New York, New York

NEW YORK LOVES FRANK

Chicago may have been "my kinda town," California is the "land I love," and the girl from Ipanema was "tall and tan and young and lovely," but no place touched Frank's heart like New York. With the bright lights and numerous night clubs, joints, and hangouts, Frank had many haunts he liked to frequent over the years. Like P.J. Clarke's on Third Avenue, a pub and burger joint where he often stayed 'til closing time at table #20 and often sang over the jukebox just for fun.

No venue was as big or important in Big Band in the 1940s than the Paramount Theatre on Broadway and Forty-Third street in New York City's Times Square.

Frank's biggest crowd to date was in 1940, as the frontman for Tommy Dorsey's band at the Paramount. They returned to play at the Paramount for a whole month a year later. And two years after that, in 1942, the Paramount was the site of his big solo debut, as well. The love affair continued for the rest of Sinatra's life and into the annals of history.

Sinatra songs about the Big Apple:

New York, New York

AUTUMN IN NY   **The Lady is a Tramp**

Brooklyn Bridge   **DOWNTOWN**

HOW ABOUT YOU   **Violets for Your Furs**

When Sinatra died, the Empire State Building was lit up in blue for three days in a silent tribute to Ol' Blue Eyes. It went blue once again to celebrate Frank's 100th birthday in 2015.

"May you live to be 100, and may the last voice you hear be mine."

—SINATRA'S FAVORITE TOAST

YANKEE PRIDE: Steinbrenner loved the song "New York, New York" so much when he heard it for the first time, he decreed it should be played at the end of every home game at Yankee Stadium. After the final game at the stadium before its renovation, the song was repeated more than two dozen times in a row as fans lingered in the stadium, refusing to leave for the last time.

Sinatra actually had TWO hits with the same name. "New York, New York" from the film *On the Town* in 1949 was sung alongside Gene Kelly and Jules Munshin. It describes the power and geography of the great city: "it's a helluva town—the Bronx is up and the Battery's down." The second hit was the iconic "(Theme From) New York, New York," which was originally performed by Liza Minnelli in the film of the same name in 1977. The tune went unnoticed until Sinatra started performing it live a year later and then recorded it on his 1980 *Trilogy* album. It went on to become the anthem of the entire city, especially after the Twin Towers were hit on September 11, 2001.

GOING SOLO IN STYLE

The First Sinatra Recordings: In 1942 while on tour with Tommy Dorsey and his big band, Frank begged Tommy to let him record a few of his songs on his own and Dorsey reluctantly agreed. Every afternoon for three weeks after, Frank honed his skills and selected his songs, rehearsing at Los Angeles's Palladium nightclub. He laid down four romantic ballads: "Night and Day," "The Night We Called It a Day," "The Lamplighter's Serenade," and "The Song Is You." When Frank first heard the recordings, he was over the moon. Alex Stordahl, his bandmate and the musician who arranged the ballads for him recalled Sinatra's reaction. "He was so excited you almost believed he had never recorded before. I think this was a turning point in his career."

SINATRA'S SOLO STAGE DEBUT

On December 30, 1942, a crisp, 30-degree winter's day, Frank opened his solo act to a sold-out crowd of adoring fans, including thousands of screaming teenage girls. Originally scheduled to run for two weeks, Frank's show was extended. His 10-week sold-out run shattered the 15-year-old record of none other than Bing Crosby. Frank's dream of eclipsing his idol's fame had come true, and he was only 27 years old.

The Columbus Day Riot of 1944: After months on the road touring and recording, Sinatra returned to NYC for a sold-out performance at the Paramount Theatre. When the morning's audience refused to leave, the afternoon crowd and all those without tickets who just wanted to get a glimpse of their idol stormed the venue. Thirty-five thousand adoring fans clashed and caused quite a stir. Hundreds of police were called in to disperse the crowds.

Being Perfectly Frank on the Radio

THE STAR-STUDDED DAYS OF LIVE RADIO

Frank was discovered on the radio, and he saw great success in the early days, as emcee, host, singer, actor, and even star of his own detective show, *Rocky Fortune*. He hosted several regular shows on NBC radio in addition to appearing live and recording albums with RCA in the early 1940s. No medium was left un-aired for Frank Sinatra as he began his meteoric rise to unparalleled stardom. He could be heard alongside greats of the era like Jack Benny, George Burns and Gracie Allen, Lucille Ball, Humphrey Bogart, Judy Garland, and any other name, big or small, who passed through the New York studios at NBC.

Everyone's Favorite Radio Host: At the same time, Sinatra was also hosting his musical performance show, *To Be Perfectly Frank*, on NBC. Billed as "Lots of music, couple a words," Frank acted as deejay and host, spinning favorite artists like Ella Fitzgerald and Lena Horne. Sinatra also performed live on the radio, backed by a five-piece combo.

The Sultan of Swoon graced the radio waves almost constantly from his debut on WNEW from the Rustic Cabin through hosting several shows and appearing as a guest on many others. Even today, Frank has had a channel dedicated entirely to him and his music on SiriusXM, Siriusly Sinatra, since 2007. During the war years, his voice could be heard overseas on the Armed Forces Radio Service.

In 1942 Sinatra was voted the "Most Popular Male Vocalist on Radio" by fans.

Frankie Goes to Hollywood

Frank toured the country with Harry James and Tommy Dorsey's bands and hit Los Angeles a few times over the years he was on tour. Hollywood musicals were all the rage, and big bands—and their artists—were featured in many of them. In 1943, Sinatra signed a seven-year deal with RKO pictures. The deal lasted barely a year, but it launched the next phase of his career and his personal life as well.

Frank first appeared in an uncredited on-screen performance in 1941, in a light comedy titled *Las Vegas Nights* singing "I'll Never Smile Again" with the Pied Pipers and Tommy Dorsey's band. His next role was singing in a war-themed light comedy titled *Ship Ahoy*, again with Dorsey and his band. In this film, a dancer hides coded military messages in her tap dancing routines.

Radio's Exciting Romantic Vocalist...FRANK SINATRA!

Frank's first on-screen gig as a solo act after leaving Dorsey's band was thanks to his new manager Frank Cooper. He appeared in the B-movie, **REVEILLE WITH BEVERLY** singing "Night and Day."

THE MOVIE STAR NEXT DOOR

His actual acting debut came a couple years later, in 1943, in the film *Higher and Higher*. In this light romantic comedy, Frank Sinatra played himself as the next door neighbor of a group of servants, scheming to marry off the house's young maid to a wealthy man. While the film was not groundbreaking or even memorable, it marked the beginning of Frank Sinatra's on-screen acting career.

Belgian artist Guy Peellaert's contributions to the 1972 book *Rock Dreams* included a painting rendered in the style of a newspaper clipping of Sinatra departing New York to launch his film career with the headline "Frankie Goes Hollywood." Yes, that's how the 1980s British band got its name. Relax!

LARGER THAN LIFE
Frank on the Big Screen

FROM STAGE TO SCREEN: Frank Sinatra had conquered the small local stages, the radio, the Paramount and Palladium theaters of New York and Los Angeles, and phonographs around the world. Next, it was time to take over Hollywood and the big screen. Less than a year after signing with RKO, Sinatra played a benefit for the Jewish Home for the Aging in Hollywood. Louis B. Mayer, the head of MGM, was in attendance and was blown away by Sinatra's presence. He set out to woo Sinatra away from his agreement with RKO, signing a long-term $1.5-million dollar contract. This deal added to all of his other contracts made Sinatra the highest-paid person in the world.

THE MGM YEARS: He appeared alongside many Hollywood legends at MGM, including Gene Kelly in *Anchors Aweigh, Take Me Out to the Ball Game*, and *On the Town*, and with British actor Peter Lawford in *It Happened in Brooklyn*. Fans loved him right from the start, and studios were clamoring to take advantage of such a hot commodity. In the mid 1940s, with tight filming schedules taking up much of Sinatra's time, Frank didn't get much time with his family, putting a strain on his relationships with his wife, Nancy, Sr., and his children. In 1944, he moved his wife and kids out to Los Angeles in an attempt to strengthen family ties and save his marriage.

Frank and Louis B. Mayer had a wonderful relationship from the start, but their contract ended abruptly after Frank made an ill-advised gaffe, publicly mentioning Mayer's illicit affair. Mayer parted ways with Sinatra and his time at MGM came to an abrupt and unexpected end.

In a career spanning from 1941 to 1995, Sinatra was cast in sixty-four films, and appeared as a singer in many more. Frank took Hollywood just as he took New York, the radio waves, and eventually television.

The Not-So-Fabulous Fifties

THE FALL OF SINATRA: In the early 1950s, Frank was appearing at the Copacabana in New York for a long engagement, but had to cancel the last two nights due to a vocal-cord hemorrhage. His singing had put such a strain on his system that he was coughing up blood. He had to remain completely silent for a week. A difficult feat for the gregarious singer.

To add to his troubles, it became clear from his falling spot on the top charts that the Bobby Soxers were growing up. After 10 years, Frank's ground-breaking sound had settled into an old, comfortable rhythm. Rock-and-roll was on the rise and it looked like it was here to stay. The golden age of television was born, with a new heartthrob as its shining symbol: Elvis Presley.

It was time to reinvent himself, and Frank the showman was more than up for the task. It was time to show the world the swagger, charm, style, and personality behind the voice.

SPINNING OUT OF CONTROL: Frank's personal life was rapidly spinning out of control as well. Rumors of his affair with Ava Gardner had reached not only his wife, Nancy, but the tabloids as well. Gossip columnists were on the lookout for any misstep by the golden boy of radio and screen, and the more bad press

he got, the angrier Frank became, prompting occasionally violent public outbursts. Where Frank once was pursued by adoring fans, he became increasingly pursued by ill-meaning members of the press looking to report on his philandering, drinking, or possible ties to organized crime.

Record sales were declining, Frank's short-lived TV show was cancelled after two seasons, and by 1952, he had lost his three big contracts with MGM, Columbia Records, and his agent. Stormy seas with wife Ava Gardner added fuel to the fire, and in mid-summer, Frank Sinatra attempted suicide by inhaling gas from his kitchen stove. He credited his friends Jackie Gleason, Manie Sacks, and Jimmy Van Heusen with helping him through those dark times that summer. It wasn't the first or the last time Frank tried to kill himself after conflicts with Gardner. Fortunately, this was not the end for Sinatra or his long, storied career. Later that same year, while on vacation with his wife Ava, he read *From Here to Eternity* and was blown away by the story. He became determined to play the role of Private Angelo Maggio onscreen.

THE END OF A SLUMP *FROM HERE TO ETERNITY*: In 1953, Sinatra got his wish. His supporting role earned him an Academy Award for best supporting actor, and the title song, which he sang, also earned an Oscar. Critics and fans loved the film so much, the Capitol Theater in NYC had to remain open 24 hours a day just to keep up with demand. The film took in a record $80 million in its first year— that's $723 million in 2017 dollars!

Sharkskin suits, casual, convivial on-stage banter,
cigarettes and cocktails . . . the hottest acts of the day
set the tone for the era, giving it a bachelor pad,
cocktail-party atmosphere. The whole country joined in.

LAS VEGAS AND THE
Rat Pack

THE HOTTEST ACT IN VEGAS AND ACROSS AMERICA

Sammy, Dean, and Frank were impressive performers on their own, but together they packed a powerful punch that reverberates in style, culture, and music to this day. There was sleepy-eyed dreamer Dean Martin, energetic Sammy Davis, Jr., and the mesmerizing, powerful Frank Sinatra. When the Rat Pack took the stage, it was more than music. They *kibitzed*, ribbed each other, and egged each other on in an intimate way that invited audiences to share their fun. Audiences were delighted!

EARLY DAYS WITH THE RAT PACK

The group of performers had traveled in the same circles for years, and fused together often in Vegas both onstage and socially. Humphrey Bogart and his wife, Lauren Bacall, had an informal drinking club at their home which Bacall dubbed "The Rat Pack," and Sinatra was a regular guest. Frank invited some of his friends and fellow performers, Dean Martin, Joey Bishop, Sammy Davis, Jr., and Peter Lawford. There was a female element to their group as well in Angie Dickinson and Shirley MacLaine. Circling the periphery of the club were Sammy Cahn, Cesar Romero, Don Rickles, Milton Berle, and Lewis Milestone.

The original RAT PACK had the inimitable Humphrey Bogart at its helm. With his cool style, cigarette in one hand, drink in the other, he was the epitome of charm. But upon his death in 1957, Frank became the new leader of the pack.

After his career stalled briefly in the early 1950s, Sinatra retreated to Las Vegas where he performed to lukewarm crowds at hotels and casinos. But his social circles expanded to include a group of friends and fellow performers who helped carry him through the rough times and into a new era for Frank and the entire country.

"There is no such thing as a clan or pack. It's just a bunch of millionaires with common interests who get together to have a little fun." —FRANK SINATRA

Great friends onstage and off: The members of the pack supported each other and their careers. "Wither thou goest" seems to be the motto of the day for most of the time, though they each had time to pursue their own projects as well. Together they made madcap adventure movies like *Ocean's 11* and *Robin and the Seven Hoods*. Audiences picked up on the group's pure enjoyment of each other's company during performances, and they showed their appreciation at the box offices. Sinatra was back on top again.

They may have been called The Rat Pack by everyone else, but Dean, Sammy, Peter, Joey, and Frank called themselves **THE SUMMIT,** after a 1960 meeting of world leaders in Paris. Sinatra wasn't a fan of the Rat Pack distinction.

The Sands Hotel was the unofficial home of the Rat Pack. It was the home of a major recording studio and was even the setting for the film *Ocean's 11*. Frank, Sammy, and Dean even got behind the casino tables and started dealing! It was no surprise they were the most popular dealers in Vegas. In 1967, just after Howard Hughes bought the Sands, Frank's credit was cut off at the casino. He was so angry, he drove his gold golf cart through the restaurant window and moved his act to Caesar's Palace.

Frank signed with **CAPITOL RECORDS** in 1953, reinventing his style from croon and swoon to swagger and strut. His recordings had an energy and power fans had only seen hints of before, and it seemed Frank was climbing back up to the top.

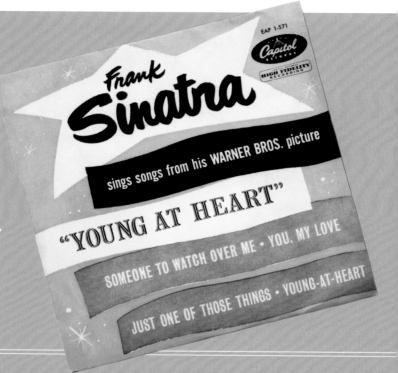

COLUMBIA RECORDS re-released Frank's earlier recordings from when he played with Harry James and his band. Columbia sales shot through the roof as Sinatramania continued to break records and reach new heights. Their re-release of the 1939 "All or Nothing at All" Frank recorded with Harry James became his first million-record seller.

Frank on Vinyl

EARLY RECORDINGS

Sinatra signed with various record labels over the years. Each label marked a different period in his career. His early years with Harry James and his orchestra were recorded with Columbia Records. His Tommy Dorsey years, Sinatra recorded with RCA. They pressed more than forty-three recordings in 1940 with the Pied Pipers, a popular singing group fronted by Jo Stafford in those days. Their recording "I'll Never Smile Again" was Frank's first #1 hit, and it was the first of many. Frank recorded a few solo tunes on the Bluebird label of RCA, but once he struck out on his own, Frank moved back to Columbia and stayed with them as a solo artist until 1952.

A CAREER REPRISE

Sinatra founded his own label, Reprise Records, in 1960 to garner more artistic freedom with his own recordings. His new corporate status led to his nickname "The Chairman of the Board." Frank had several other nicknames, some flattering, like "Slats" from his skinny boyish frame in his early years, "Ol' Blue Eyes," "The Voice," and "The Sultan of Swoon," and others not so much—like "Scarface." His new label brought him back to the top of the charts around the same time he and the Rat Pack members took over the Las Vegas stages.

In 1946, Sinatra recorded a whopping 57 songs. The following year, 1947, saw Sinatra breaking his own record, recording 71 songs in one year.

THE PERFORMER

THE TWO SIDES OF SINATRA

Sometimes tough but at other times tender, there were two sides to Sinatra that were present in everything he did on stage and off. His wistful tenderness had a rough edge, and his hard-edged swagger wasn't so hard that he didn't let his softer side through. His early performances in the 1940s as he was just coming to the forefront were all lighthearted, whether it was in films like *Anchors Aweigh* or *On the Town*, or in the songs he recorded back then like "Night and Day" and "The Song is You."

As Sinatra matured and the country moved away from its wartime distraction of lighthearted entertainment, he was still cast in lighthearted fun films, like *High Society* and *Guys and Dolls*. But he was also placed in demanding and complex roles like the politically charged film *The Manchurian Candidate*, his exciting adventures with the Rat Pack with *Ocean's 11*, and his Academy Award-winning performance in *From Here to Eternity*.

PRACTICE ALWAYS MADE PERFECT FOR FRANK

His vocal range was equally impressive. He took cues from every performer he admired, like Bing Crosby's crooning, Gene Kelly's dancing, and Dorsey's stamina and control. Frank worked his hardest to emulate his idols, outstrip them, and beat them at their own game as singers and also as performers. Although Sinatra couldn't match Gene Kelly's dance steps, he worked as hard as he could so he didn't look awkward on stage next to the dancing superstar. Sinatra took great pains to expand his already expansive vocal range and practice his breath control so even when he belted out the heart of a song, it still seemed effortless.

"He was a skinny runt — but then he opened his mouth, and it was awesome." —GENE KELLY

Frank had a unique mixture of swagger and vulnerability that drew people in and kept them listening. His warm, inviting, Italian way of singing directly to the heart of everyone listening was a far cry from the polished crooners of an earlier age, who sang as if it was their job. Frank Sinatra breathed life into the words of the song, conveying their meaning as well as the tune.

The Men Behind the Man and the Music

Sinatra worked closely with many of the songwriters whose music and words made him famous. **JULE STYNE**, who wrote "Saturday Night (Is the Loneliest Night of the Week)," "I Fall in Love Too Easily," and "Guess I'll Hang My Tears Out to Dry," once received a gift from Sinatra—a gold bracelet engraved with "To Jule Who Knew Me When." Styne and Sinatra also shared a love of baseball. Jule played alongside Nat King Cole and many others on Sinatra's amateur team of all-stars, The Sinatra Swooners.

> "I fall in love too easily, I fall in love too fast."
>
> — Frank Sinatra as Clarence Doolittle in *Anchors Aweigh*, MGM 1945

AXEL STORDAHL was arranging songs for Tommy Dorsey when Sinatra joined the band. It was clear from the start that the arrangements and the singer worked in perfect harmony together. Naturally, when Sinatra broke out with his first solo recordings, Stordahl was the one doing the arrangements. They continued on together for the next decade, creating the award-winning music for Sinatra's duets with Gene Kelly in *Anchors Aweigh*.

WHO NEEDS A BAND? In 1943, the musician's strike was still going strong. Frank found himself in a Columbia Records recording studio with the Bobby Tucker Singers and no orchestra. They sang together a cappella and put together beautiful renditions of "You'll Never Know," "Close to You," and "People Will Say We're in Love."

> **"What he is singing about has nothing to do with the Rat Pack, martinis, cigars, and golf, and everything to do with the essence of what it means to be human."**
>
> —STEPHEN HOLDEN, MAY 17, 1998,
> *THE NEW YORK TIMES*

In the early 50s when Sinatra's career was in a slump, it was his recording with **NELSON RIDDLE**, "I've Got the World on a String," that put Sinatra back on top. Sinatra and Riddle and the Nelson Riddle Orchestra recorded and performed together for the next 10 years. He worked with Sinatra and Bing Crosby in the acclaimed musical *High Society*.

QUINCY JONES took Sinatra through the 1960s, arranging and conducting Sinatra's album *It Might as Well Be Swing* with Count Basie, and *Sinatra at the Sands*, also with Basie. Jones was called upon once more when Count Basie and Sinatra teamed up for a television special filmed at *The Hollywood Palace* in 1965. Sinatra left Quincy Jones his iconic ring, which Jones treasures and never takes off.

Hitting the Charts

THE MAGIC OF MODERN TECHNOLOGY

The album *Duets* (and its aptly named sequel *Duets II*) paired Sinatra with younger singers in all different genres. Aretha Franklin, Barbra Streisand, Julio Iglesias, Gloria Estefan, Tony Bennett, Natalie Cole, Charles Aznavour, Carly Simon, Liza Minnelli, Anita Baker, Bono, and Kenny G all sang duets with Sinatra. The first album sold more than three million copies in the United States, earning it triple-platinum status. But the most interesting thing about the album, historically, isn't the wide range of pairings but in how it was produced. Sinatra arranged and performed each of the songs in a studio with the orchestra, then had the artists sing alongside his recording and send it back. The duet artists were never actually in the same room as each other. LeRoy Neiman painted a specially commissioned portrait for the cover, which ironically, considering the name Duets, features a solo Sinatra singing alone.

Frank recorded "Somethin' Stupid," a duet with daughter Nancy, in 1967. The president of Reprise Records was unimpressed and bet Frank $2 that the tune would flop. When it hit #1, he framed the promised $2 bill, which Nancy still has. To date, "Somethin' Stupid" is the only father-daughter duet to hit #1 on the U.S. *Billboard* Hot 100 chart.

FRANK SINATRA

A Hollywood Star 3x Over: Sinatra has three stars on the Hollywood Walk of Fame. At 1600 Vine Street for his work in the movies, at 1637 Vine Street for his records, and at 6538 Hollywood Boulevard for his television work.

A-NUMBER-ONE: "(Theme From) New York, New York" was Frank Sinatra's final Top 40 chart hit. Despite its success, the songwriters were displeased with his rendition, in which he ad-libbed lyrics like "A-number-one."

WWII

His Own Medal of Honor

Sinatra had always been outraged by racial and ethnic discrimination. He kept hearing reports from Europe of Nazi treatment of the Jews, and was frustrated he couldn't join his fellow Americans at the front in their fight against injustice. Sinatra had a special medallion made. On one side was a St. Christopher medal, on the other was a Star of David. He wore one himself and gave the rest away to friends.

DECEMBER 7, 1941: The Japanese bombed Pearl Harbor, bringing war close to home. Frank was among the first to be drafted, but due to a punctured eardrum during his traumatic birth, he was classified 4-F, unfit to serve. This devastated Sinatra, a strong patriot who desperately wanted to do his part for his country. He tried over the years to enlist to do his part, but never succeeded.

Not everyone believed Frank's 4-F classification. William Randolph Hearst and his conservative newspapers weren't big fans of (at the time) the left-leaning Sinatra or his support of Roosevelt. Hearst's publications embarked on a smear campaign to discredit Sinatra, accusing him of dodging military service and intimating that he had ties to organized crime. Because of the bad press, Sinatra was denied a visa to entertain troops overseas during the war. After V-E day, Frank finally got permission to head overseas. He boarded a plane, along with fellow performer Phil Silvers, to entertain the troops in celebration of their victory.

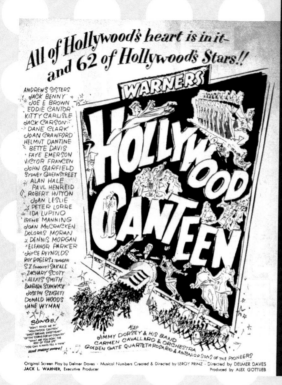

All of Hollywood's heart is in it— and 62 of Hollywood's Stars!!

WARNER'S

HOLLYWOOD CANTEEN

ANDREWS SISTERS
JACK BENNY
JOE E BROWN
EDDIE CANTOR
KITTY CARLISLE
JACK CARSON
DANE CLARK
JOAN CRAWFORD
HELMUT DANTINE
BETTE DAVIS
FAYE EMERSON
VICTOR FRANCEN
JOHN GARFIELD
SYDNEY GREENSTREET
ALAN HALE
PAUL HENREID
ROBERT HUTTON
JOAN LESLIE
PETER LORRE
IDA LUPINO
IRENE MANNING
JOAN McCRACKEN
DOLORES MORAN
DENNIS MORGAN
ELEANOR PARKER
JOYCE REYNOLDS
ROY ROGERS & TRIGGER
S.Z. (CUDDLES) SAKALL
ZACHARY SCOTT
ALEXIS SMITH
BARBARA STANWYCK
JOSEPH SZIGETI
DONALD WOODS
JANE WYMAN

SONGS! "DON'T FENCE ME IN" "HOLLYWOOD CANTEEN" "SWEET DREAMS SWEETHEART" "GETTIN' CORNS FOR MY COUNTRY" "WHAT ARE YOU DOIN' THE REST OF YOUR LIFE" "YOU CAN ALWAYS TELL A YANK"
And many more!

ALSO JIMMY DORSEY & HIS BAND CARMEN CAVALLARO & ORCHESTRA GOLDEN GATE QUARTET ROSARIO & ANTONIO SONS OF THE PIONEERS

Original Screen Play by Delmer Daves · Musical Numbers Created & Directed by LEROY PRINZ · Directed by DELMER DAVES
JACK L. WARNER, Executive Producer   Produced by ALEX GOTTLIEB

Throughout 1944, Sinatra toured the states, singing to servicemen and performing for them at the Hollywood Canteen as well. The enlisted men loved his music and performances as much as the Bobby Soxers did! Somehow, Sinatra managed to keep up his radio shows and filming schedules with MGM while doing his part supporting the troops.

Sinatra's failure to enlist landed him on the path to success. While the troops were overseas, Frank's romantic love ballads captured the attention of all those left behind back at home, pining for their loved ones.

POW! RIGHT IN THE KISSER: In 1947, Sinatra was arrested for the second time. This time for slugging a journalist for a Hearst newspaper. Sinatra popped Lee Mortimer in the jaw in response to Mortimer's accusations of Frank's alleged ties to the Mob. Mortimer and Sinatra had been in a long-time feud, with Mortimer publishing allegations of communism and draft-dodging in the conservative Hearst newspapers. When it all came to a head, Mortimer insulted Sinatra's Italian heritage with name-calling and that was enough to push Sinatra over the edge.

Sinatra
THE REBEL

Because of his feuds with the conservative press, Frank was voted the Hollywood Women's Press Club "Least Cooperative Star" of 1946.

Frank Sinatra was on top of the world in the 1940s.
He had it all: he was the biggest star on record, with recording contracts, radio shows, a movie contract, hordes of fans, and an adoring wife and kids, too. Frank worked long hours, often went without sleep, and drank and smoked to excess. The hard living eventually took its toll on his voice by the end of the decade, and Sinatra started showing signs that he couldn't keep up the pace he had set for himself professionally or musically.

HIS WAY

Frank started to act as though he lived by his own set of rules. He was often seen spending time with known members of the organized crime scene. In 1947, Sinatra shocked and disappointed fans everywhere when he briefly left his wife, Nancy, and their two children at the time for Hollywood bombshell Lana Turner. He also spent a fair amount of time with the ladies, including actress Marilyn Maxwell.

CELEBRITIES, SCANDAL, AND THE MOB

JUST ANOTHER DAY IN LAKE TAHOE

The classic Calneva Resort, built in 1926 on the border of California and Nevada in Lake Tahoe, was the site of Sinatra's failed suicide attempt in 1951. But the hotel made the news again in 1960 when the owners received an offer they couldn't refuse. The resort was bought by Chicago mobster Sam Giancana along with Frank Sinatra and Dean Martin. The hotel received a major upgrade such as a helipad and a celebrity room, and drew notable personalities including Marilyn Monroe, the Kennedy family, Judy Garland, members of the Rat Pack, and members of the American Mafia. The casino lost its gambling license due to its tolerance of the Mafia presence, and Sinatra sold the resort in 1968.

Marilyn Monroe spent her last troubled weekend at the resort, where she had a failed suicide attempt.

IN 1962, Mobster Sam Giancana used his muscle to force the Rat Pack to perform at the Villa Venice club in Chicago.

CAMELOT AT CALNEVA: The Kennedy family had their own set of rooms where the FBI and reporters kept tabs of the affairs, possible Mob connections, and social lives of the Kennedy family members. Sinatra and the Kennedys were close, even earning him a White House invitation in the early days of the Kennedy administration. Sinatra introduced mobster Sam Giancana to the Kennedys, giving the Mob direct access to the White House. But after Sinatra's ties to the Mob were publicized in the media, the Kennedy family withdrew, keeping their distance from Sinatra's scandal-ridden persona.

Frankie AND THE MOB

BERGEN COUNTY
SHERIFF'S OFFICE
11 27 38
42799

Arrested! You've seen the iconic image of his 1938 mug shot, but what was it for? An old girlfriend accused him of leading her on and promising to marry her. The charges were initially for "seduction," then were changed to "adultery" before they were dropped. The woman was already married.

Great Expectations: Sinatra's fascination with the world of organized crime is no secret to the public. The FBI kept a huge dossier on him, following his connections with known Mob bosses and reporting on conversations with informants. The dossier was released upon his death, revealing no incriminating evidence of any crimes.

"I think that he's always nurtured a secret desire to be a 'hood'."

—BING CROSBY IN AN INTERVIEW WITH *COSMOPOLITAN* IN 1956

THE *GODFATHER* INCIDENT

Was Mario Puzo's character Johnny Fontane in the 1969 novel *The Godfather* based on Frank Sinatra? Fontane's character was a famous crooner who used his Mob connections to break into Hollywood. He also recruited a few of his friends involved in organized crime to help him get out of a contract. Was this based on Frank Sinatra's Hollywood career and feud with Tommy Dorsey? Frank seemed to think so.

THE BACKSTORY: Bandleader Tommy Dorsey took young Frank under his wing and helped elevate him to superstardom, that much is clear. Frank was grateful to Dorsey for the opportunities he presented, the doors he opened, and most of all the musical education he gave Frank. On stage, Frank studied Dorsey's amazing showmanship and also his lung capacity—his ability to hold a note for 8 or even 16 bars, depending on who's telling the story—without appearing to take a breath. Sinatra reported that he took up swimming and running to increase his lung capacity. More likely, as he did with everything else he attempted, young Sinatra simply kept practicing so he could keep up and surpass the person who inspired him.

When Frank gave notice ten months before his three-year contract was out so he could pursue his solo career, Dorsey felt angry and betrayed. Sinatra wanted out. Rumors flew that he recruited some muscle to force Dorsey's hand, but several other rumors, from a simple cordial handshake to a roomful of lawyers, have also been claimed as the truth. Either way, Sinatra was angry and told Puzo to his face on more than one occasion. Puzo denied it, but the truth may never really come to light. However the story actually went, all accounts end pretty much the same way . . . with Dorsey's final words to Frank when he quit the band: "I hope you fall on your ass."

A SOCIAL, POLITICAL, AND LEGAL MENACE:

Over the years, Sinatra was considered a potential social, political, and legal menace, corrupting the youth, communing with communists, and promoting racial equality, not to mention consorting with members of organized crime syndicates. The FBI reported investigating a claim that Sinatra forged his 4-F papers to avoid the draft, and routinely looked into claims printed in the gossip columns, no matter how outlandish they seemed. The files included details of Sinatra's outspoken support of democratic groups that were tied to communist suspicions and groups supporting racial harmony—along with reports that Sinatra may have beaten up cafe owners who wouldn't serve the black members of his band.

THE SINATRA FILES

AN OPEN BOOK: Upon Sinatra's death, the press insisted the FBI open up their secret files on the man, the myth, and the legend, under the Freedom of Information Act. In 1998, the files were released. His dossier was a whopping 1275 pages. In 1943, the feds started keeping tabs on Sinatra based on a letter that suggested that fans' mass hysteria for Sinatra was similar to the crowds supporting Adolf Hitler. The letter-writer suggested fans could see the parallel and begin supporting Hitler, or even worse, could turn the American singer into a version of Hitler in the United States.

THE MOB: It was only a matter of time before those reports also included Sinatra's ties to organized crime. Sure enough, the files mention Mob giants Lucky Luciano, Bugsy Siegel, and Mickey Cohen, with specific dates, and details of conversations. From suspected ties to local New Jersey crime boss Willie Moretti to an offer from Bugsy Siegel to come sing at the opening of the Flamingo Hotel in Las Vegas, the reports are detailed but not very conclusive. In fact, Sinatra wasn't brought up on any charges from all of the surveillance over forty years.

SINATRA OFFERED TO HELP THE FBI: In 1950, it seemed Sinatramania was coming to an end. Released from his contracts, his voice strained, and his popularity waning, Sinatra went to the FBI and offered to do his part for his country by opening up communications with people of interest. The FBI—even Hoover himself—wanted nothing to do with him.

THE FBI HELPS SINATRA: In July of 1964, Frank, Jr., was kidnapped and the FBI put aside any issues the bureau might have had with the Chairman of the Board to help secure his son's safe release.

SINATRA'S
Bad Reputation

BAD PRESS: William Randolph Hearst was no fan of President Roosevelt, nor was he a fan of the liberal political actions of Frank Sinatra. Hearst took every opportunity to smear Roosevelt and his famous supporters. Starting in 1947 and continuing for years, Hearst begin a crusade against Sinatra, spreading lies and rumors, calling out possible ties to the Mob, and manipulating facts intended to lead to Sinatra's downfall. Sinatra was no fan of the press and had run-ins with some of Hearst's employees who often used unethical tactics to find a story and try to catch Frank in the act.

HIS WAY: Kitty Kelley wrote a "tell-all" unauthorized biography of Sinatra, titled *His Way*, by interviewing people who knew him well, including his daughter, Tina, as well as those involved with Sinatra's life at one point or another. Kelley alleges Mafia ties, tantrums, bad behavior, and more based on these interviews. Sinatra, his family, and several of his close friends tried desperately to stop the book from being published because it defamed Sinatra's character as well as that of many of his close friends and associates. The book was published and widely read. The public was shocked. Some believed what they read and saw Frank in a new light. Many others simply compared the corrupt version of Sinatra to the purity of his voice and sincerity in his songs and chose to believe their ears instead.

"I'd rather be a don for the Mafia than President of the United States"

—EDDIE FISHER RECALLED SINATRA SAYING

"I've been a puppet, a poet, a pauper, a pirate, a pawn and a king; I've been up and down and over and out, and I know one thing: Each time I find myself flat on my face I pick myself up and get back in the race."

September of His Years

So Long Solo: Sinatra's solo album in 1965 was balanced with notable collaborations throughout the 1960s, including three with Count Basie. Sinatra and Count Basie recorded *Sinatra-Basie* in 1962, *It Might As Well Be Swing* in 1964, and *Sinatra at the Sands* in 1966. The 1966 album was recorded in the Copa Room at the Sands Hotel and Casino in Las Vegas and was arranged by Quincy Jones.

1966—IT WAS A VERY GOOD YEAR: 1965 marked Sinatra's fiftieth birthday. He attacked his career with a new enthusiasm and maturity. His 13-song solo album *September of My Years* balanced a mixture of nostalgia with introspection and optimism and the result was a poignant and vulnerable look at the man behind the voice for anyone who cared to look deeper. The album won a Grammy Award for Album of the Year, and the hit single "It Was a Very Good Year" won for best male vocal performance in 1966.

SEEING THE SINGER IN THE SONG: Always a study in contrast, Sinatra recorded the almost flippant devil-may-care themed "That's Life" the following year. It received lukewarm reception from many critics but still received gold-selling status. While the music is as memorable as it is easy and fun to listen to (very), it's the lyrics that, in hindsight, are the most telling about the singer.

RETIREMENT
AND COMEBACK

1971 SINATRA RETIRES! Frank grew tired of performing the same songs to the same audiences, and who could blame him. He had taken the country through many cultural revolutions from the Depression through World War II, a slump in the fifties, through the physically exhausting and trend-setting Rat Pack years. Frank deserved a break. After a final rendition of "That's Life," he stated simply "Excuse me while I disappear," and walked off the stage.

OL' BLUE EYES IS BACK: Ever the marketing genius, Sinatra staged his return with a bang. He released the album *Ol' Blue Eyes is Back* in 1973, which hit #13 on the *Billboard* charts. He starred on TV in a special reuniting with Gene Kelly, and embarked on an ambitious world tour through the United States, Europe, the Far East, and Australia.

STUMPING FOR NIXON IN CHICAGO: Sinatra briefly came out of retirement in 1972 to sing at a Nixon rally in Chicago. His tune, not surprisingly, was "My Kind of Town."

FRANK AND THE AUSTRALIAN PRESS: The pressure of the paparazzi was too much for Sinatra, and he lashed out at the Australian journalists who were closing in on him from all fronts. He launched a tirade at them, calling the lot of them "bums, parasites, fags, and buck-and-a-half hookers," and had to publicly apologize in a final performance before he left Australia.

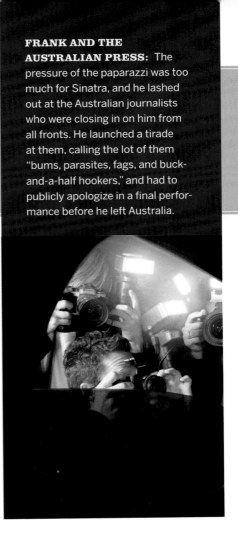

Frank approached all of his roles the same way he sang— he performed to the heart of the voice, whether he was portraying a character or singing a ballad, and made the audience believe and feel every word.

THE SMALL SCREEN

THE FRANK SINATRA SHOW: Sinatra made the inevitable transition to television with *The Frank Sinatra Show* in 1951. The musical variety show on CBS was sponsored by Bulova, watches and featured guest spots with Hollywood giants like Milton Berle, Jack Benny, Jackie Gleason, and Sarah Vaughan. He was also joined onstage by his old singing buddies The Pied Pipers from his Tommy Dorsey days. Fans enjoyed the comedy antics and performances, but the show was canceled after the second season. Fans liked Sinatra, but his energy that worked so well on stage, radio, and in movies seemed pent up and constrained by the small screen television format.

THE FRANK SINATRA SHOW REDUX

In 1957, ABC bet that the world was ready for Sinatra to return to TV and that they had the perfect recipe. They paid Sinatra $3 million for 39 episodes: 13 variety shows, 13 dramas starring Sinatra himself, and 13 dramas with Frank as the host. Frank shone in the variety shows, but grew impatient with the dramas. ABC finally cut its losses after 32 episodes and closed the curtain on Sinatra's bids for TV series for good.

A Man and His Music

Sinatra's fiftieth birthday celebration was a public affair—broadcast in full color on television. Frank sang in a TV studio in front of a live audience, accompanied by the Nelson Riddle Orchestra and introduced by Ed McMahon. The show was sponsored by Budweiser and was recorded and released on vinyl as well. *A Man and His Music* received an Emmy Award for Outstanding Musical Performance. Two more specials followed in 1966 and 1967, the first featuring his daughter Nancy, and the second featuring Ella Fitzgerald and Antonio Carlos Jobim.

Welcome Home, Elvis: Sinatra was not a fan of rock-and-roll music. He claimed it led young people to destructive and bad behavior. An ironic twist as many adults remembered the disruptive behavior caused by the Bobby Soxers during the early Sinatramania days! But when Elvis Presley returned from his military service, Sinatra was right there to welcome him home publicly on television. The reason probably boiled down to ratings—two of music's biggest stars together for one night only was guaranteed to be a blockbuster hit. Even so, Sinatra had his Rat Pack buddies by his side on stage.

What Sinatra Stood For
HIS POLITICS AND BELIEFS

THE FILM THAT TAGGED SINATRA A COMMUNIST

Sinatra didn't keep quiet about the things he believed in. In 1944, he refused to join a country club when he learned they did not accept Jews. In 1945, he made a short film called *The House I Live In*, speaking out in favor of racial and religious acceptance.

His performance earned him a special Academy Award.

Six months later, he was tagged as a potential communist.

"Look, fellas, religion makes no difference except to a Nazi or somebody as stupid. Why, people all over the world worship God in different ways. This wonderful country is made up of a hundred different kinds of people, and a hundred different ways of talking, and a hundred different ways of going to church. But they're all American ways. My dad came from Italy, but I'm an American. Should I hate your father 'cause he came from Ireland or France or Russia? Wouldn't I be a first-class fathead?"

—SINATRA, AS HIMSELF, *IN THE HOUSE I LIVE IN*

The House I Live In wasn't Sinatra's only tie to communism. He was very public about his call for racial harmony. The 1940s were a racially charged time, where de-facto segregation was de rigeur, but Frank didn't leave a single man behind due to race, creed, or color, and was even reported to have beaten more than one cafe owner who refused to serve members of his party while traveling in the South.

"I believe in you and me. I'm like Albert Schweitzer and Bertrand Russell and Albert Einstein in that I have a respect for life—in any form. I believe in nature, in the birds, the sea, the sky, in everything I can see or that there is real evidence for. If these things are what you mean by God, then I believe in God. But I don't believe in a personal God to whom I look for comfort or for a natural on the next roll of the dice."

—SINATRA, *PLAYBOY* INTERVIEW, 1963

A Young Democrat, but an Old Republican

A devoted Democrat when he was young, he named his son Frank, Jr., "Franklin" for Franklin Delano Roosevelt. His rendition of "High Hopes" was the anthem of the Democratic party when JFK was running for president. But by 1985, however, he was such a staunch conservative, he proudly produced Ronald Reagan's Inaugural Gala and often performed benefits to help out fellow Hollywood veteran Reagan's campaign.

MCCARTHYISM HITS HOME: In 1949, Senator McCarthy and the House Un-American Activities Committee set its sights on Hollywood. As a supporter of civil rights and the Democratic party, Sinatra was called out for following and helping the Communist party line. While Sinatra's career wasn't affected by the accusations, many of his friends in Hollywood were. He tried to support his friends emotionally, financially, and in their careers as their lives were destroyed by McCarthyism.

"If you don't know the guy on the other side of the world, love him anyway because he's just like you. He has the same dreams, the same hopes and fears. It's one world, pal. We're all neighbors."

—SINATRA, *PLAYBOY* INTERVIEW, 1963

Strange but True

SINATRA HATED "MY WAY" MORE THAN HE HATED "STRANGERS IN THE NIGHT": "My Way" was originally a French tune. Paul Anka wrote new English lyrics. It became Sinatra's signature tune despite the fact that he apparently hated the song. Close friend Shirley MacLaine revealed that Frank was a deeply humble man and was embarrassed by the braggadocio lyrics.

HE SANG THE SONGS, NOT THE NOTES: Sinatra never learned to read music, despite the fact that he arranged, composed, and sang his way to superstardom.

A FAMILY BUSINESS: Frank's wife made his trademark soft, floppy bow ties when he first went solo. Fans kept ripping them right off his neck and taking them as souvenirs. Nancy, Sr., had to make new ones by the dozens but she couldn't keep up with the demand! Nancy was also in charge of all of Frank's fan mail until his agent finally took over. Nancy and her sisters would autograph his pictures for hours every night, address the envelopes and send them out to unsuspecting fans who thought they were getting something personal from Frank himself.

MAMA KNOWS BEST: Frank often said his favorite cook was his mother. He shared his favorite recipe for her tomato sauce with the world by launching his own line of tomato sauce in the 1980s.

"I COULDN'T SLEEP A WINK LAST NIGHT": According to legendary jazz drummer Buddy Rich, with whom Sinatra shared hotel rooms on the road when they were touring with Dorsey's band, Frank was an insomniac who stayed up most nights reading . . . and clipping his toenails in the hotel room at 2:00 a.m.

A LOVER AND A FIGHTER: Sinatra got into his share of fistfights over the years, but he also got involved in a couple of prize fights. He backed Floyd Patterson to beat Ali, and when Patterson lost, Sinatra never spoke to him again. Fast forward to 1971, The Fight of the Century was on the books and tickets were hard to come by, even for The Chairman of the Board. Always resourceful, Sinatra scored a press pass to cover the fight for *Life* magazine and scored a front row seat.

FRANK WAS ONCE STRUNG UP BY HIS BOWTIE ON STAGE BY CRAZED FANS: At the end of a performance at the Paramount Theatre in 1941, crazed Bobby Soxers grabbed hold of Frank's necktie at either end as the retractable stage was receding. Singer Connie Haines recalled poor Frank was hanging there, suspended by his bowtie as the stage floor was being pulled out from underneath him. Connie and Tommy Dorsey quickly fought off the girls and helped him make a clean getaway.

THE FRANK SINATRA SCHOOL FOR THE ARTS, a public high school for young artists, was founded by Tony Bennett and his wife, Susan Benedetto, as a tribute to Tony's best friend. The school is based in Tony's hometown of Astoria, Queens, minutes away from the heart of Manhattan.

A SHOW OF SUPPORT: Sinatra starred in one of the first American films to openly discuss the issue of homosexuality, *The Detective*, in 1968.

FRANK SINATRA WAS ONLY 5´7˝ but elevator shoes enhanced his larger-than-life appearance!

THE GENTLEMAN'S DRINK: Frank's signature drink was made with four ice cubes, two fingers of Jack Daniel's, a splash of water. Always served with a cocktail napkin.

ROCK-AND-ROLL ON THE BOSS: Introducing the man who needed no introduction, Bono once said "Frank never did like rock-and-roll. And he's not crazy about guys wearing earrings either. But he doesn't hold it against me. And anyway, the feeling is not mutual. Rock-and-roll people love Frank Sinatra because Frank has got what we want: swagger and attitude. He's big on attitude. Serious attitude, bad attitude. Frank's the Chairman of the BAD. Rock-and-roll plays at being tough but this guy, well, he's the boss."

A SAD FAREWELL: Sinatra's mother died in a plane crash on her way to see her son's opening night performance at Caesar's Palace in Las Vegas in 1977.

A TRUE STAR: 7934 Sinatra is an asteroid named after The Chairman of the Board. The heavenly body was discovered in 1989 and was promptly named to keep the torch lit for this shining star after his death.

SINATRA THE PITCHER: Growing up, he was a huge Brooklyn Dodgers fan. In the late 1940s, Sinatra sponsored his own softball team, The Swooners, featuring a star-studded lineup of actors, musicians, and industry giants. Frank played second base along with songwriters Jule Styne and Sammy Cahn, and actors Anthony Quinn, Hank Sanicola, and Barry Sullivan. They were supported by a gorgeous team of cheerleaders: Virginia Mayo, Shelley Winters, Marilyn Maxwell, and Ava Gardner.

PHILANTHROPY

Deeds Large and Small

Stardom may have gotten to Sinatra's head many times over the years, but his compassion and kindness were legendary in their own way. He performed many big benefits over the years, performing for the troops, performing to raise money for war bonds, making appearances for charities, and lowering his fees at struggling venues. But his humanity wasn't limited to large-scale deeds. According to Frank's daughter, Nancy, Jr., Frank once sent sandwiches to forty fans in the audience at the Paramount Theatre whom he recognized as coming back to see him six and seven times in a row. Frank witnessed another young fan get her hand caught in a door as he was leaving a recording studio. He sent his manager back to see if the little girl was okay, then treated her to ice cream.

Frank and his fourth wife Barbara founded the **Barbara Sinatra Children's Center in Rancho Mirage**, California. The center, founded in 1986, provides therapy and support to children victimized by abuse. Frank used to visit the center and read to the children, but his most significant contributions were financial.

"In Nancy I found beauty, warmth and understanding; being with her was my only escape from what seemed to be a grim world."

—FRANK SINATRA

Love and Marriage

Frank Sinatra was married four times, but was also a notorious womanizer. For Frank, love and marriage didn't quite go together like a horse and carriage, as the song went. Frank was twice as passionate and mercurial in his love affairs as he was in his songs that sent half the country into a heated frenzy.

First Love. Frank met his first wife, Nancy Barbato, in 1935 when vacationing with his family on the Jersey Shore. At the young age of nineteen, Frank was smitten with Nancy, who was seventeen. He serenaded her on her front porch with his ukulele and they began to date. They married four years later, in 1939, and had three children together.

Nancy knew of Frank's philandering. Just before they were married, Frank was arrested on morality charges for having an affair with a married woman. One of his dalliances was with Lana Turner. Frank spent a lot of time boozing and cavorting throughout the 1940s, and by 1949, Frank's exploits were well-known in their private circles and in the tabloids, and it was taking a toll on his singing performances as well. Frank was in a career slump and his personal relationships weren't going well, either. It was his relationship with Ava Gardner that ultimately led to his divorce in 1951. Six days after the divorce papers were signed, Frank and Ava were married.

SAILING THE STORMY SEAS WITH AVA

His second marriage to actress Ava Gardner lasted from 1951 to 1953. Frank and Ava had a passionate relationship. They were alternately lovers and fighters, but rarely anything in between.

When Sinatra and Gardner split, Frank was hit hard and even contemplated suicide. His musical recordings, however, showed more fire and passion than ever before. This time, Frank channeled his feelings into his singing, and what resulted was pure gold.

As for their breakup? Sinatra summed up his sad mood in one sentence: "It was all Mondays."

"The troubles were all out of bed—the quarreling started on the way to breakfast." —FRANK SINATRA

Frank's name was tied to other major stars in the firmament of cinema at the time, Marlene Dietrich and Marilyn Monroe, who also had their own personal demons to wrestle with as their outward careers flourished and shone brightly.

Frank once again threw himself into a series of stormy relationships. He reportedly proposed to Peggy Connelly, then Lauren "Betty" Bacall right after the death of her husband and his close friend Humphrey Bogart. The mid-1950s was a series of unmemorable one-night-stands for Frank, whose then-signature torch song of loneliness, "One for the Road," was a perfect mirror of his life at the time.

MIA FARROW

Raised in Beverly Hills, Mia Farrow is the daughter of Hollywood legends Maureen O'Sullivan and John Farrow. Her breakout role was on *Peyton Place* at the age of nineteen. She married Sinatra in 1966 at the age of twenty-one. When fellow Rat Packer Dean Martin learned of Frank's intention to marry Mia, who was thirty years his junior, he quipped that the groom had "bottles of Scotch older than his bride!" They were only married for two years before Farrow took on her iconic role in *Rosemary's Baby* in favor of working with her husband on his film *The Detectives*. He served her divorce papers on set. Farrow never got over Sinatra. They remained close friends and lovers. When Farrow came to Sinatra upset over Woody Allen's relationship with her adopted daughter and alleged abuse of her younger daughter, Frank was there to offer support and possibly even send over some tough guys to take care of him, according to several reports.

SINATRA MARRIED ZEPPO MARX'S EX-WIFE

His final marriage was to Barbara Blakely Marx in 1976. Marx was a former model and Vegas showgirl, but the couple didn't meet while Frank was working the Vegas scene. Barbara and her husband Zeppo Marx, of the Marx Brothers comedy team, were close friends and neighbors of Sinatra. She had fallen in love with his voice on the radio as a girl growing up in Missouri, and even briefly married an aspiring singer when she was young. By the time Barbara and Frank met, Barbara was already married to Zeppo and was a high-profile staple of the Palm Springs social scene. She left Zeppo Marx for Frank in 1973, but he didn't propose until she threatened to leave if he didn't put a ring on it. Sinatra's marriage to Barbara was his longest-lasting relationship. They remained together until he died. She passed away in July of 2017.

THE FAMILY MAN

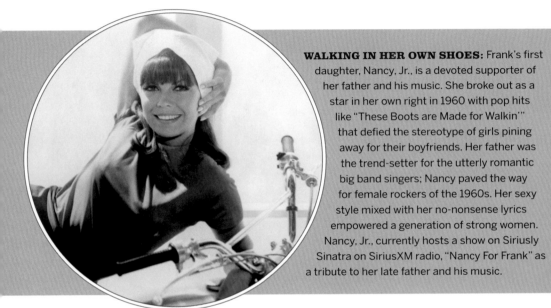

WALKING IN HER OWN SHOES: Frank's first daughter, Nancy, Jr., is a devoted supporter of her father and his music. She broke out as a star in her own right in 1960 with pop hits like "These Boots are Made for Walkin'" that defied the stereotype of girls pining away for their boyfriends. Her father was the trend-setter for the utterly romantic big band singers; Nancy paved the way for female rockers of the 1960s. Her sexy style mixed with her no-nonsense lyrics empowered a generation of strong women. Nancy, Jr., currently hosts a show on Siriusly Sinatra on SiriusXM radio, "Nancy For Frank" as a tribute to her late father and his music.

A FOURTH SINATRA? There are several reports that Mia Farrow's son Ronan may have been Frank's, not her then-husband, Woody Allen's. While this hasn't been substantiated, Ronan is close with the Sinatras and has always been treated like family. Nancy, Jr., also remains close with her former stepmom Mia, and thinks of her as more of a sister than anything else.

IN HIS FATHER'S FOOTSTEPS: Frank, Jr., always lived in his father's shadow, despite his successful career. Occasionally while performing on stage, he would introduce a medley of his father's songs, saying: "I am now going to devote five minutes to the music of Frank Sinatra because that is exactly how long Frank Sinatra devoted to me." He died in 2016 at age seventy-two.

KIDNAPPED! In December 1963, Frank's son, Frank Sinatra, Jr., (a performer in his own right) was kidnapped from his Lake Tahoe dressing room. His father paid the $240,000 ransom, but before the FBI could track the money via the serial numbers, a brother of one of the kidnappers contacted the police. He defended himself by saying, "You just don't mess with someone like Frank Sinatra."

CHRISTINA "TINA" SINATRA: When Tina was born, Frank was on the road and on his way out of the family's life. Her parents split when she was just a baby, so she never had the opportunity her older siblings had to experience life sharing the spotlight—or being in the shadow—of her father. Tina wasn't very interested in singing and pursued acting briefly, including a few TV roles. She was in the pilot TV movie *Fantasy Island*, which became a long-running Saturday night favorite in the seventies. Tina was an agent and also produced a few television shows honoring her father. She wrote a book about her family life, *My Father's Daughter*, in 2000.

Friends

Family life in Hollywood in the mid-1940s was going swimmingly for the Sinatras. They had a private house on a lake where they could enjoy each other's company and get away from it all. In town, Sinatra lived a more typical Hollywood lifestyle, hobnobbing with other movie stars. Sinatra was introduced to many movie greats in 1945 who would become his lifelong friends: Bing Crosby, Jack Benny, Phil Silvers, Lauren Bacall, and Humphrey Bogart. He also struck up a friendship with Ava Gardner, who was married to Mickey Rooney at the time. After Frank's divorce from Nancy years later, Ava would become his second wife and the catalyst for his stormier days.

STANDING IN FOR RAGS

Sinatra and Phil Silvers were old friends from before they toured Europe entertaining troops. In 1946, Silvers was planning a big performance at the Copacabana with his old friend Rags Ragland when Rags died suddenly, three weeks before the performance. On opening night, Silvers was preparing to go onstage alone and grieving, when his old pal Sinatra showed up ready to perform.

May 14, 1998

FRANK SINATRA DIED ON MAY 14, 1998, IN LOS ANGELES after a severe heart attack. His wife, Barbara, was by his side. His last words were "I'm losing."

His funeral on May 20 in Beverly Hills was attended by 400 friends and celebrities but there were thousands of fans outside the church paying tribute to the man who gave so much to so many.

Frank was buried with items his family felt were meaningful. At his funeral, Nancy, Nancy, Jr., and Mia dropped cherry Life Savers, Tootsie Rolls, stuffed toys, a, dog biscuit, a bottle of Jack Daniels, Camel cigarettes, a Zippo lighter, a note, Mia's wedding ring, and a dime into his casket. Why the dime? He always told his family never to go anywhere without one. "You never know who you'll have to call."

Frank Sinatra willed the arrangements of his songs to Steve Lawrence. His will had a no-contest clause that said anyone who contested it would be left out completely.

On his tombstone, his epitaph reads:
"The Best is Yet to Come." That was also the
title of the last song he sang in public.

Awards and Achievements

> "I would like to be remembered as a man who had a wonderful time living life, a man who had good friends, fine family—and I don't think I could ask for anything more than that, actually."

—FRANK SINATRA IN A 1965 INTERVIEW WITH WALTER CRONKITE

RECORDING ACADEMY AWARDS

Frank was awarded the Grammy Lifetime Achievement Award in 1966 as well as eight additional Grammy Awards. He received thirty-one nominations throughout his singing career. In 1959, at the first ever annual Grammy Awards, Sinatra was nominated six times and won, not for his voice or music but for his art direction on the album cover of *Only the Lonely*. He received the Trustees Award in 1979, and was awarded a Grammy Legend Award in 1995.

> "I saw Sinatra and the Pope on TV when I was two and said, 'Who's that guy with Frank Sinatra?'" —ROSEANNE BARR

Oscar-Winning Dramatic Performance: Won Best Supporting Actor at the Academy Awards in 1953 for his portrayal of Private Angelo Maggio in *From Here to Eternity*.

In Color Across America: Awarded a 1966 Peabody Award for *A Man and His Music* a one-hour television special in color, on NBC.

Honored by the White House: Presented with the Presidential Medal of Freedom, the highest civilian award in the U.S. by his friend President Ronald Reagan in 1985.

Recognition of Service: A 1983 honoree at the Kennedy Center Honors for his charitable work, championing causes related to childhood illnesses and abuse.

MAJOR AWARDS IN FILM, TV, AND MUSIC

1953, Oscar
Best Performance by an Actor in a Supporting Role

1954, Golden Globe
Best Performance by an Actor in a Supporting Role in a Motion Picture

1958, Golden Globe
Best Performance by an Actor in a Motion Picture—Musical or Comedy

1958, Grammy
Best Album Cover

1959, Grammy
Album of the Year

1959, Grammy
Best Male Pop Vocal Performance

1965, Grammy
Album of the Year

1965, Grammy
Best Male Pop Vocal Performance

1966, Grammy
Record of the Year

1966, Grammy
Album of the Year

1970, Oscar
Jean Hersholt Humanitarian Award

1971, Golden Globe
Cecil B. DeMille Award

1972, Screen Actors Guild Awards
Life Achievement Award

1995, Grammy
Best Traditional Pop Vocal Performance

1966, Grammy
Best Male Pop Vocal Performance

SINATRA FIRSTS

First radio broadcast 1935

The Mills Brothers song "Shine" on *Major Bowes and His Original Amateur Hour* radio show.

First on-screen appearance 1935

The short films *The Night Club and The Big Minstrel Act* with the Hoboken Four, produced by Major Bowes. In *The Night Club*, he played a waiter. In *The Big Minstrel Act*, he performed in a blackface singing troupe.

First Album 1939

Just two weeks after his debut performance with Harry James and his orchestra, Sinatra cut his first record, *From the Bottom of My Heart*.

First big audience 1940

Frank sang with Tommy Dorsey's band at the biggest, most popular big band venue in the country, New York's Paramount Theatre.

First #1 1940

"I'll Never Smile Again," was the first Dorsey/Sinatra record to hit number one.

First full-length film appearance 1941

In *Las Vegas Nights* with the Tommy Dorsey Orchestra

First songwriting credit 1941

"This Love of Mine," co-authored with music by Sol Parker and Hank Sanicola for RCA records.

First singles recorded without a big band 1942

"Night and Day" / "The Night We Called It a Day" and "The Lamplighter's Serenade" / "The Song Is You"

First on-screen kiss 1944

Anne Jeffreys in *Step Lively*

First non-musical acting role 1948

The Miracle of the Bells for RKO pictures. Frank played a priest and audiences were unconvinced.

First stereo recording 1953

"Three Coins in the Fountain" became a major pop-chart hit and went on to win the Academy Award for Best Music for an Original Song.

FILMOGRAPHY

1941 *Las Vegas Nights* as Singer

1942 *Ship Ahoy* as Himself

1943 *Reveille with Beverly* as Frank Sinatra

1943 *Higher and Higher* as Frank Sinatra

1944 *Step Lively* as Glenn Russell

1945 *Anchors Aweigh* as Clarence Doolittle

1946 *Till the Clouds Roll By* as Specialty Performer in finale

1947 *It Happened in Brooklyn* as Danny Webson Miller

1948 *The Miracle of the Bells* as Father Paul

1949 *The Kissing Bandit* as Ricardo

1949 *Take Me Out to the Ball Game* as Dennis Ryan

1949 *On the Town* as Chip

1951 *Double Dynamite* as Johnny Dalton

1952 *Meet Danny Wilson* as Danny Wilson

1953 *From Here to Eternity* as Angelo Maggio

1954 *Suddenly* as John Baron

1954 *Young at Heart* as Barney Sloan

1955 *Guys and Dolls* as Nathan Detroit

1955 *Not As a Stranger* as Alfred [Boone]

1955 *The Tender Trap* as Charles Y. Reader

1956 *Around the World in 80 Days* as Pianist at Barbary Coast Saloon

1956 *High Society* as Mike Connor

1956 *Johnny Concho* as Johnny Concho

1956 *Meet Me in Las Vegas* as Man at Slot Machine (uncredited)

1956 *The Man with the Golden Arm* as Frankie Machine

1957 *Pal Joey* as Joey Evans

1957 *The Joker Is Wild* as Joe E. Lewis

1957 *The Pride and the Passion* as Miguel

1958 *Kings Go Forth* as Lt. Sam Loggins

1959 *A Hole in the Head* as Tony Manetta

1959 *Never So Few* as Capt. Tom C. Reynolds

1959 *Some Came Running* as Dave Hirsh

1960 *Can-Can* as François Durnais

1960 *Ocean's 11* as Danny Ocean

1961 *Invitation to Monte Carlo* as Himself

1961 *Pepe* as Himself

1961 *The Devil at 4 O'Clock* as Harry

1962 *Sergeants 3* as 1st Sgt. Mike Merry

1962 *The Manchurian Candidate* as Bennett Marco

1962 *The Road to Hong Kong* as The 'Twig' on Plutomium (uncredited)

1963 *4 for Texas* as Zack Thomas

1963 *Come Blow Your Horn* as Alan Baker

1963 *The List of Adrian Messenger* as Gypsy

1964 *Paris When It Sizzles* as Themselves [voices]

1964 *Robin and the 7 Hoods* as Robbo

1965 *Marriage on the Rocks* as Dan Edwards

1965 *None but the Brave* as Chief Pharmacist's Mate Maloney

1965 *Von Ryan's Express* as Col. Joseph L. Ryan

1966 *Assault on a Queen* as Mark Brittain

1966 *Cast a Giant Shadow* as Vince

1967 *The Naked Runner* as Sam Laker

1967 *Tony Rome* as Tony Rome

1968 *Lady in Cement* as Tony Rome

1968 *The Detective* as Joe Leland

1970 *Dirty Dingus Magee* as Dingus Magee

1974 *That's Entertainment!* as Narrator

1977 *Contract on Cherry Street* as Deputy Inspector Frank Hovannes

1980 *The First Deadly Sin* as Edward Delaney

1984 *Cannonball Run II* as Himself.

1986 *The Spencer Tracy Legacy* as Himself

1988 *Who Framed Roger Rabbit* as Voice of Singing Sword

1989 *Entertaining the Troops* as Himself

1990 *Listen Up: The Lives of Quincy Jones* as Himself

1995 *Young At Heart* as Himself

DISCOGRAPHY

1947	*The Voice of Frank Sinatra*	Legacy/Columbia
1950	*Swing and Dance With Frank Sinatra*	Columbia/Columbia/Legacy
1953	*Requested by You*	CBS Records
1954	*Swing Easy!*	Capitol/Universal
1954	Songs for Young Lovers	Capitol/Universal
1955	*The Voice*	Balboa Recording Corporation
1955	*In the Wee Small Hours*	EMI-Capitol Entertainment Prop./Capitol
1956	*Songs for Swingin' Lovers!*	Capitol/EMI Records/Capitol
1956	*High Society*	Back Biter
1956	*Frank Sinatra Conducts Tone Poems of Color*	Capitol
1957	*Pal Joey* [Original Soundtrack]	Capitol
1957	*Where Are You?*	Capitol/EMI Records/Capitol
1957	*Close to You and More*	Capitol/EMI Records/Capitol
1957	*A Swingin' Affair!*	Capitol
1957	*A Jolly Christmas from Frank Sinatra*	Capitol/EMI Records/Capitol
1958	*Only the Lonely*	Capitol
1958	*Come Fly with Me*	Capitol/EMI Records/Capitol
1959	*No One Cares*	Capitol/EMI Records/Capitol
1959	*Come Dance with Me!*	Capitol/EMI Records/Capitol

1960	Nice 'n' Easy	Capitol/EMI Records/Capitol
1960	Can-Can [Original Soundtrack]	Capitol
1961	Sinatra's Swingin' Session!!! And More	Alliance
1961	Swing Along with Me	Reprise
1961	Ring-a-Ding Ding!	Reprise/Universal
1961	Come Swing with Me!	Capitol/EMI Records/Capitol
1961	Point of No Return	Capitol
1961	Frank Sinatra Conducts Music from Pictures and Plays	Reprise
1962	Sinatra & Strings	Reprise
1962	All Alone	Reprise
1962	Sinatra & Sextet: Live in Paris	Reprise
1962	Sinatra-Basie: An Historic Musical First	Reprise
1962	Sinatra and Swingin' Brass	Reprise/Universal
1962	Sinatra Sings Great Songs from Great Britain	Reprise
1963	The Concert Sinatra	Reprise
1963	I Remember Tommy	Warner Bros.
1963	Sinatra's Sinatra: A Collection of Frank's Favorites	Reprise
1964	It Might as Well Be Swing	Reprise
1964	Days of Wine and Roses, Moon River and Other Academy Award Winners	Reprise/Warner Bros.

1964	*Robin and the 7 Hoods*	Artanis Entertainment Group
1964	*Softly, As I Leave You*	Signature Sinatra/Universal
1964	*Guys and Dolls* [Reprise Musical Repertory Theatre]	Warner Bros.
1964	*America, I Hear You Singing*	Signature Sinatra/Universal/ Universal International
1965	*September of My Years*	Reprise
1965	*Sinatra '65*	Signature Sinatra/Universal
1965	*My Kind of Broadway*	Reprise
1965	*Moonlight Sinatra*	Reprise
1966	*Sinatra at the Sands*	Reprise
1966	*That's Life*	Signature Sinatra/Universal
1966	*Strangers in the Night*	Signature Sinatra/Universal
1967	*Francis A. & Edward K.*	Reprise
1967	*Francis Albert Sinatra & Antonio Carlos Jobim*	Signature Sinatra/Universal
1967	*The World We Knew*	Signature Sinatra/Universal
1968	*The Sinatra Family Wish You a Merry Christmas*	Artanis Entertainment Group
1968	*Cycles*	Reprise
1969	*Watertown*	Signature Sinatra/Universal
1969	*My Way*	Reprise
1969	*A Man Alone: The Words & Music of McKuen*	WEA International

1971	*Sinatra & Company*	Reprise
1973	*Ol' Blue Eyes Is Back*	Reprise
1974	*The Main Event: Live*	Reprise
1974	*Some Nice Things I've Missed*	Reprise
1980	*Trilogy: Past, Present & Future*	Reprise
1981	*She Shot Me Down*	Signature Sinatra/Universal
1984	*L.A. Is My Lady*	Qwest
1986	*A Man and His Music*	Signature Sinatra/Universal/ Universal International
1993	*Duets*	Capitol/EMI Records/Capitol
1994	*Duets II*	Capitol/EMI Records/Capitol
1998	*Rat Pack Collection* [Madacy]	Madacy

PHOTO CREDITS